D1525588

ZORA NEALE HURSTON

ZORA NEALE
HURSTON
HARLEM RENAISSANCE WRITER

KERSHAW COUNTY LIBRARY
WITHDRAWN
632 W. DeKalb St. Suite 109
Camden, South Carolina 29020

by Katie Marsico

Content Consultant:
Dr. Kathryn L. Seidel, Professor
Department of English, University of Central Florida

ABDO
Publishing Company

CREDITS

Published by ABDO Publishing Company, 8000 West 78th Street, Edina, Minnesota 55439. Copyright © 2008 by Abdo Consulting Group, Inc. International copyrights reserved in all countries. No part of this book may be reproduced in any form without written permission from the publisher. The Essential Library™ is a trademark and logo of ABDO Publishing Company.

Printed in the United States.

Editor: Nadia Higgins
Copy Editor: Paula Lewis
Interior Design and Production: Emily Love
Cover Design: Emily Love

Library of Congress Cataloging-in-Publication Data
Marsico, Katie, 1980–
  Zora Neale Hurston / Katie Marsico.
    p. cm. — (Essential lives)
  Includes bibliographical references.
  ISBN 978-1-60453-036-0
  1. Hurston, Zora Neale—Juvenile literature. 2. Novelists, American—20th century—Biography—Juvenile literature. 3. Folklorists—United States—Biography—Juvenile literature. 4. African American novelists—Biography—Juvenile literature. 5. African American women—Biography—Juvenile literature. I. Title.
  PS3515.U789Z783 2008
  813'.52—dc22
  [B]
                                        2007030840

TABLE OF CONTENTS

Zora Neale Hurston, left, returned to her hometown of Eatonville, Florida, to collect southern black folklore.

THE LURE OF THE
LYING SESSIONS

t was February 1927, and the warm southern sun was a refreshing change for writer Zora Neale Hurston. She had only recently left the harsh winter of Harlem, New York. Hurston drove her used Ford—which she had affectionately nicknamed Sassy Susie—through her hometown of Eatonville, Florida. She was delighted to see that not much had changed.

Tropical fruits and flowers still perfumed the air, and social boundaries and stereotypes that existed in so many other parts of the country were generally invisible. Eatonville was the first U.S. community to be officially founded and run by African Americans, and its population was entirely black. Though Hurston had traveled to northern cities to find work and get an education, she never forgot the warmth and vitality of the Eatonville townsfolk. Most of all, she recalled the excitement and creativity of the "lying sessions"on the front porch of Joe Clarke's store.[1]

As a child, Zora had passed several happy afternoons listening to the men exchanging fabulous folklore. Their amazing tales involved everything from God and the creation story to animals that walked upright and took on human

Any Excuse to Eavesdrop

When Zora lived in Eatonville, Joe Clarke's store was considered a gathering place for adults. Children were not encouraged or permitted to join in grown-up conversations or even listen to the tall tales being told. Zora, however, was intrigued by the magical quality of the folklore spun on the front porch, so she found clever ways to spend as much extra time there as she could. As she later recalled, "I was not allowed to sit around there naturally. But I could drag my feet going in and out whenever I was sent there for something to allow whatever was being said to hang in my ear."[2]

personalities. She adored these fantastic accounts and looked to them to shape her own childhood stories and games. She later recalled,

> No doubt, these tales of God, the devil, animals, and natural elements seemed ordinary enough to most people in the village. But many of them stirred up fancies in me. ... Life took on a bigger perimeter by expanding on these things. I picked up glints and gleams out of what I heard and stored it away to turn to my own uses.[3]

It was these "glints and gleams" that lured Hurston back to Joe Clarke's porch in 1927. Now an accomplished college student and a blossoming writer, she had not merely returned to Eatonville for a pleasant visit with old friends. She was home on business. Under the guidance of a favorite anthropology professor at Barnard College in New York City, she was being paid $1,400—a generous amount at that time—for her work. She was to spend about six months collecting the "stories, superstitions, songs, dances, jokes, customs, and mannerisms of the black South."[4]

Unfortunately, the mission in Eatonville did not turn out to be as simple or as successful as Hurston had initially imagined. In the years since she had left town, she had gained a formal education and vast exposure to the African-American cultural movement known as the Harlem Renaissance. She was quite different from the girl who had once clamored to hear more tall tales. Though residents were welcoming, most had never earned a college degree or even left Eatonville. Villagers sensed the distinction that set this worldly young woman apart from everyone else.

Like Hurston, they also had a difficult time regarding her homecoming as

A Dangerous Drive

Hurston's tour of the South in 1927 was a bold move, especially since she frequently traveled alone. She had to be cautious of areas and people that were not always welcoming to African Americans. At the time she visited the region, many southern states had legislation known as Jim Crow laws that denied fair treatment to people of color. For example, restaurant owners were required to provide separate entrances for black and white customers and to seat them out of view from each other.

Even more dangerous, however, was the ever-present threat of physical harm. It was not uncommon for a white mob to lynch an African American who they believed had committed some wrongdoing. This meant that the mob killed the victim—usually by hanging—without consulting authorities or having any kind of a trial.

Hurston was aware of the challenges and perils she faced as she drove through the backwoods of Florida and nearby states. However, she was not one to be terrified by racism or to be so upset by it that she lost sight of her mission. "Sometimes I feel discriminated against," she acknowledged, "but it does not make me angry. It merely astonishes me. How can any deny themselves the pleasure of my company! It's beyond me."[5]

"A Feather-bed Resistance"

Shortly after arriving in Eatonville in 1927, Hurston realized that it would be a challenge to get townspeople to open up to her and share their knowledge of local folklore.

She described her interviews with Eatonville residents as "a feather-bed resistance. That is, we let the probe enter, but it never comes out. It gets smothered under a lot of laughter and pleasantries."[7] Hurston realized that, while members of the community were gracious and enjoyable to talk to, they did not readily reveal the same kind of amazing stories that she had once heard at Joe Clarke's store.

part of her research. Hurston was eager to indulge in familiar, entertaining stories and to enjoy the company of the storytellers. Yet her anthropology professor had instructed her not to get lost in the magic and genius of the plots. She was to pay closer attention to the manner in which tales were relayed and songs were sung. In the end, Hurston discovered, "Folklore is not as easy to collect as it sounds." She noted, "Oh, I got a few little items. But compared with what I did later, not enough to make a flea a waltzing jacket."[6] As the world would learn, what she did later would indeed be remarkable.

LIMITLESS TALENT, LIMITING TIMES

Hurston was destined to gain acclaim for her brilliance as an author and her bold, unconventional attitudes in both the literary world and everyday society. She lived in an era when vast numbers of African Americans labored for little money and lived in fear of discrimination and violence. But Hurston pushed past financial hardships and an unstable family life to attend school and establish herself as a writer. Ultimately, she achieved recognition for her work as an anthropologist, a journalist, a dramatist, and the author of several short stories and novels.

Yet Hurston's world was by no means carefree, even after she became famous. In spite of her success, she faced the harsh judgment and misconceptions of a segregated society. When Hurston made her trip to Eatonville in 1927, many people still did not place much value in what African Americans—or women— had to offer.

Even after she was an established author, not everyone approved of or appreciated the way she portrayed African Americans in her writing. Hurston wanted to explore black culture and to

The Pride of Eatonville

Eatonville residents continue to proudly claim Hurston as one of their own. Since 1989, the town has hosted an annual Zora Neale Hurston Festival of the Arts and Humanities. This event celebrates the "cultural contribution which Africa-descended people have made to the United States and to world culture."[8] Eatonville is also home to the Zora Neale Hurston National Museum of Fine Arts and the Zora Neale Hurston Youth Institute.

depict well-rounded, realistic characters who experienced hope and success, as well as sorrow and failure. Some critics argued that her choice of dialogue mocked how African Americans spoke. Others, including members of her own race, insisted that she did not focus enough on the suffering of her people. In her defense, Hurston explained that the world needed to see African Americans as men and women whose lives involved issues beyond discrimination and prejudice. As she noted, "It is urgent to realize that the minorities do think, and think about something other than the race problem."[9]

Hurston's own existence demonstrated the truth behind this statement. In 69 years of life, she experienced heartbreak and scandal as well as great excitement and adventure. Despite her success as an author, money was often tight. Yet Hurston never gave up her passion for writing. The slender, free-spirited woman who rolled into Eatonville in Sassy Susie was the same storyteller who eventually became famous for creating "literature in every best sense of the word."[10]

Zora Neale Hurston at a book fair in 1937

African-American children play a singing game in Eatonville, Florida.

ROOTS OF A REMARKABLE
IMAGINATION

When Zora was born on January 7, 1891,
African Americans had been officially
free from slavery for only about 28 years. And
despite their recent liberation, few were able to enjoy

the full benefits of U.S. citizenship—particularly in southern states. Many African Americans were all too familiar with discrimination and oppression. They often were unable to attend the same schools as whites, use the same public facilities, or even seek protection under the same laws.

People of color also were faced with limited job opportunities, and many were employed as domestic laborers, such as housekeepers or sharecroppers. As sharecroppers, they rented land from a plantation owner and paid the rent with a portion of the crops they grew. No matter what their jobs were, African Americans generally earned little money, struggled with poverty, and regularly faced unfair laws and attitudes that restricted their rights.

Zora's father, John Hurston, envisioned something greater for himself and his family. Self-educated, he found it limiting to work as a sharecropper on other people's cotton plantations. He and wife Lucy Anne Potts already had four other children—Bob, John, Richard, and Sarah—when they welcomed Zora into the segregated world of Notasulga, Alabama. John saw a promising alternative to this life in Eatonville, which is about five miles (8 km) north of Orlando, Florida.

In the 1890s, many African Americans struggled as sharecroppers. The Hurstons found an escape from such hardship in Eatonville.

ESCAPING TO EATONVILLE

An all-black town run by an all-black government, Eatonville was founded in 1887 and was unique for the late nineteenth century. Because of its racial makeup, prejudice was virtually nonexistent. Most residents worked on citrus farms or cooked and cleaned on nearby white estates. Yet the village offered an atmosphere of equality and potential that did not exist for African Americans in most other parts of the nation.

This environment proved prosperous for the Hurstons. After moving to Eatonville, John established a successful carpentry business, gained recognition as a Baptist minister, and helped create some of the town's laws. Lucy worked as a seamstress and taught Sunday school. The couple had three more children—Clifford, Benjamin, and Everett— between 1893 and 1898. The family eventually built an eight-room, two-story house on five acres (2 ha) of land made even more picturesque by chinaberry and gardenia trees and jasmine bushes.

In Zora's eyes, Eatonville was a community filled with sunshine, citrus fruits, alligators, and limitless material just perfect for a little girl with an ever-turning mind. It was a place where people of her skin color were encouraged to succeed and be happy and where they had the freedom and the means to actually do so. Zora's upbringing in Eatonville would shape her attitudes about race and her fierce sense of determination for years to come.

Lucy also played a critical role in shaping her daughter's driven personality. A former teacher, she actively assisted her children in the evenings with their school lessons. Like so many other Eatonville residents, Lucy believed that skin color

Child of the Chinaberry Trees

As an adult, Hurston traveled from the southern backwoods to glamorous northern cities to the Caribbean islands. As she explained in her autobiography, her longing to explore was present from early childhood.

The strangest thing about it was that once I found the use of my feet, they took to wandering. I always wanted to go. I would wander off in the woods all alone, following some inside urge to go to places. This alarmed my mother a great deal. She used to say that she believed a woman who was an enemy of hers had sprinkled "travel dust" around the doorstep the day I was born.[1]

As a girl, Zora liked to sit in a chinaberry tree in her front yard and chat with passersby. Eager to make conversation, sometimes she would accompany them for a short distance before returning home. From her perch, she dreamed of adventures in far-off places. She wished that she, too, could wander down the lane to new destinations. She later remembered,

The most interesting thing I saw [from the chinaberry tree] was the horizon. Every way I turned, it was there, and the same distance away. Our house then, was in the center of the world. It grew upon me that I ought to walk out to the horizon and see what the end of the world was like.[2]

should neither define one's accomplishments nor serve as an excuse for failure. As Hurston reflected in her autobiography, "Mama exhorted her children at every opportunity to 'jump at de sun.' We might not land on the sun, but at least we would get off the ground."[3]

A Sassy Tongue and a Spectacular Mind

Zora's mother encouraged her to pursue her dreams, but her father did not express the same enthusiasm for his fifth child. "He predicted dire things for me," Hurston later recalled. "I was going to be hung before I got grown. Somebody was going to blow me down for my sassy tongue."[4] Hurston always contended that, already having one daughter by the time she was born, her father was disappointed she was not a boy. A strict disciplinarian, Zora's father had little patience for his second-

Least-Favorite Child

Zora forever insisted that she was her father's least-favorite child. "It seems that one daughter was all that he figured he could stand," she explained. "My sister, Sarah, was his favorite child, but that one girl was enough. Plenty more sons, but no more girl babies to wear out shoes and bring in nothing. I don't think he ever got over the trick he felt that I played on him by getting born a girl."[5]

eldest daughter's daydreaming and tall tales.

Yet Zora could not stop herself from gobbling up literature and folklore, whether she was exposed to it at school or more informally around her neighborhood. She particularly enjoyed fairy tales and myths spun by Roman, Greek, and Norwegian peoples of the past. Whether she read about Hercules or the characters of Hans Christian Andersen, she found herself stirred to explore her own imagination.

The stories told over checkers games or in between bits of local gossip at Joe Clarke's store only added to this inspiration. Though she may not have realized it as a young girl lingering to hear one last colorful account, the manner in which the townspeople spun folklore also ultimately had an impact on Zora. Their words

A Box of Books

Though an all-black town during the late 1800s, Eatonville was not without its share of white visitors. These men and women were mainly missionaries, philanthropists, or travelers making their way to Orlando. At about the time Zora was in fifth grade, two such ladies were guests at her school. They were so impressed with the way Zora recited her lesson that they remembered her after they departed Eatonville. Later on, they shipped her gifts of clothes and books. As Zora recalled, "The books gave me more pleasure than the clothes. ... In that box [were] *Gulliver's Travels*, *Grimm's Fairy Tales*, *Dick Whittington*, *Greek and Roman Myths*, and best of all, *Norse Tales*."[6]

and how they spoke them were a reflection of the southern black culture. It was a culture that Hurston would be determined to celebrate with her writing.

As a child, however, Zora knew only that she was spinning tales of her own. Her fabulous accounts involved people transformed into alligators and talking lakes. Sometimes her stories featured characters based on everyday objects, such as Mr. Sweet Smell (soap) or Miss Corn-Shuck. With such a far-reaching sense of make-believe, Zora discovered she had no need for dolls and store-bought toys. As she explained,

> When inanimate things ceased to commune with me like natural men, other dreams came to live with me. Animals took on lives and characteristics which nobody knew anything about except myself. Little things that people did or said grew into fantastic stories.[7]

Toys Too Limiting

When Zora was a child, she found she preferred playing with everyday household objects rather than dolls and other store-bought toys. As she explained, "Dolls caught the devil around me. They got into fights and leaked sawdust. … They jumped off the barn and tried to drown themselves in the lake. Perhaps the dolls bought for me looked too different from the ones I made up myself. The dolls I made up in my mind did everything. Those store-bought things had to be toted and helped around. Without knowing it, I wanted action."[8]

Unfortunately, Zora's childhood fantasy world was destined to be rocked by a painful reality. At 13, she was hit hard with a devastating loss that cut her carefree existence short and tested her already difficult relationship with her father. ⌐

Zora Neale Hurston in 1903

*A Ku Klux Klan member displays a hangman's noose in
an attempt to intimidate African Americans.*

LEARNING HARSH
LESSONS

Zora's mother, Lucy, had always been the one who shielded Zora from her father's judgment. If John considered his youngest daughter too bold and bright for her own good, it was Lucy who sought to protect and nurture those qualities. The parents' differing attitudes when it came to Zora were sometimes the source of heated debates in the Hurston home. As Zora recollected,

My mother was always standing between us [Zora and her father]. She conceded that I was impudent and given to talking back, but she didn't want to "squinch my spirit" too much for fear that I would turn out to be a mealy-mouthed rag doll by the time I got grown.[1]

September 1904 saw Lucy a changed woman. Always somewhat delicate, her health suffered after returning from a trip to Alabama to visit her dying sister. Lucy took to her bed and passed away on September 18. Though only 13, Zora realized immediately that her life would never be the same. "Mama died at sundown and changed a world. … We were all grubby bales of misery, huddled about lamps."[2]

Regrettably, Lucy's death did not bring Zora and her father closer together. Though both grieved deeply, John offered little comfort to his child. It was only a matter of weeks before Zora was sent away to attend school with older siblings Bob and Sarah at Florida Baptist Academy in Jacksonville, Florida.

Thrust into a Segregated Society

For a confident, creative child who had grown up in the accepting, open-minded village of Eatonville, Jacksonville presented a shock to Zora's sense of identity. A major southern city, it was filled with both whites and blacks, and the social boundaries between the two groups were more clear-cut than anything the teenager had yet experienced. As Zora put it, "Jacksonville made me know that I was a little colored girl. Things were all

A Promise Broken

At the time Zora's mother passed away, the South was teeming with superstitions about death. Common traditions included covering clocks and mirrors in the dying person's room. It was believed that a dying person's glance could make a clock stop working or alter a mirror's reflective powers. Custom also demanded that any pillows be removed from under the dying person's head, as this was thought to make their final moments easier.

Lucy, however, was insistent that these measures not be carried out at her death, and she begged young Zora to promise that her final wishes be fulfilled. Unfortunately, the people of Eatonville did not lightly disregard such customs. So, John and several local women covered the mirror and clock and removed the pillow from under Lucy's head while Zora desperately protested from across the room.

Her inability to keep her promise to Lucy haunted Zora for many years:

> That moment was the end of a phase in my life, I was old before my time with grief of loss, of failure, or remorse of failure. No matter what the others did, my mother had put her trust in me. ... And then in that sunset time, I failed her. ... That hour began my wanderings. Not so much in geography, but in time. Then not so much in time as in spirit.[3]

about the town to point this out to me."[4]

Whereas Eatonville residents had made her feel like she was capable of accomplishing her dreams, the citizens of Jacksonville flooded Zora's mind with a different message. She was black, and she was a girl. There were limits to what she could do with her life, and it was best to accept this and not stir up trouble. No matter how intelligent she was or how much potential she demonstrated, her new world would only allow her to excel to a certain point.

Fortunately, this sudden exposure to prejudice did not stop Zora from quickly proving herself a talented student. However, her sharp tongue and outspoken spiritedness tried the patience of certain members of the staff at Florida Baptist Academy. Sometimes, this also made it hard for her to fit in with the other boys and girls. She may not have been

An Awful Bother

Florida Baptist Academy granted John's request to enroll Zora there in the fall of 1904, although at 13, she was still two years younger than most of her classmates. Zora quickly demonstrated that her age did not affect her abilities as a student, but she found it more difficult to make friends. "Around the school I was an awful bother," she later recalled in her autobiography. "The girls complained that they couldn't get a chance to talk without me turning up somewhere to be in the way."[5]

Jacksonville, Florida, in the early 1900s

miserable, but she was homesick and sorely missed her mother's companionship. Hurston later remembered, "School in Jacksonville was one of those twilight things. It was not dark, but it lacked the bold sunlight that I craved."[6]

Tuition payments were also a source of constant stress. School officials were quick to make Zora aware that her father had failed to send enough money to meet the costs of her education. To earn her keep, Zora scrubbed stairs and worked in the kitchen.

In February 1905, her father married a woman named Mattie Moge, and the bride was in no way enthusiastic about her new stepchildren. As the school year drew to a close in 1905, John made no arrangements for his daughter's return to Eatonville. Finally, a member of the staff took pity on Zora and paid for part of her traveling expenses to Eatonville. The young girl began the journey back to a "house which was no longer home."[7]

A Discouraged Drifter

Mattie and Zora were almost instantly at odds with one another, and John frequently took his new wife's side in what became constant battles. As time wore on, the situation worsened. The Hurston children entered into physical struggles with their unpopular stepmother. When the atmosphere became completely unbearable, Zora left home. She did not know how she would survive or to whom she could turn in an unfriendly, unfamiliar world.

Little is known about this period of her life, but Hurston once described it by saying,

The five years following my leaving the school at Jacksonville were haunted. I was shifted from house to house of relatives and friends and found comfort nowhere. … I was miserable, and no doubt made others miserable around me because they could not see what was the matter with me, and I had no part in what interested them.[8]

Home No More

When Zora returned home from Jacksonville in 1905, she immediately noticed a deeply sorrowful change in the home where she had enjoyed so many happy childhood memories. "The very walls were gummy with gloom," she recollected. "Too much went on to take the task of telling it. Papa's children were in his way because they were too much trouble to his wife. Ragged, dirty clothes and hit-and-miss meals. The four older children were definitely gone for good. One by one, we four younger ones were shifted to the homes of Mama's friends."[9]

Between 1906 and 1911, Zora found herself working at domestic jobs in various parts of Florida and occasionally attending classes for brief periods of time. Unfortunately, school had a price tag attached to it, and she hardly earned enough to buy decent clothes. She encountered difficulty finding work because of her youthful appearance and small build—people wanted big, strong maids who were older and more experienced. What employment Zora did secure was generally short-lived. She was hired to clean for wealthy, white homeowners but was ultimately let go. Zora was more interested in reading the families' books or playing with the children than doing chores.

Zora continued to float from job to job, barely managing to stay one step ahead of poverty. She briefly returned home around 1911, but she and her stepmother continued to attack one another—on one occasion to the point of bloodshed. Not long after, she traveled to Nashville, Tennessee, to help her brother Bob and his wife with their growing family while he studied to become a doctor. She quickly grew impatient with Bob's empty promises to send her back to school. As Hurston later recounted,

> I wanted to get through high school. I had a way of life inside me and I wanted it with a want that was twisting me. And now it seemed I was just as far off as before.[10]

Reading instead of Dusting

Zora's love of literature and make-believe did not stop simply because her early education came to a halt after 1905. Unfortunately, these affections often got in the way of her domestic work. "I did very badly," she explained, "because I was interested in the front of the house, not the back. No matter how I resolved, I'd get tangled up with their reading matter and lose my job. It was not that I was lazy, I just was not interested in dusting and dishwashing. But I always made friends with the children if there were any. … That would be fun, but going out to play did not help much on jobs."[11]

An escape from her unfulfilling existence was not as distant as Zora imagined, however. She was no longer a sheltered, sassy little girl who could scale the chinaberry trees of Eatonville. But she was a driven, creative young woman who remained determined to jump for the sun—no matter how impossible or impractical society made that seem.

DUST TRACKS ON A ROAD

By

Zora Neale Hurston

To

***

The James Weldon Johnson Memorial Collection of Negro Arts and Letters at Yale University through the efforts of Carl Van Vechten to enrich it.

Zora Neale Hurston.

Los Angeles, California
January 14, 1942.

Parts of this manuscript were not used in the final composition of the book for publisher's reasons.

Zora Neale Hurston.

*In 1941, Hurston would reflect on her youth in her autobiography,
Dust Tracks on a Road.*

The main building at Howard University in Washington, D.C.,
where Hurston began her college education

Eager for an Education

y 1915, Zora Hurston was 24 years old
and living in Memphis, Tennessee. She
had experienced nearly 11 years of disappointment
and discouragement filled with people telling her

she could not do this or would never be able to do that. It was, therefore, a welcome relief when she was offered work as a maid for the lead singer of the Gilbert and Sullivan theater company. Her salary was far greater than it had ever been before, and she was thrilled by the adventurous life the actors seemed to lead.

In turn, the white members of the company enjoyed the colorful way Hurston spoke, and they appreciated her bright mind. Much to her delight, the actors and singers lent her books. They exposed her to the thrill of drama and the charm of short, engaging musical performances known as light opera.

For many years, Hurston had been forced to set aside her natural love of reading and learning; now it was suddenly reawakened in her. Just as importantly, she was again inspired to accomplish the goals that so many people considered too elevated for a poor, black orphan to pursue. In 1917, Hurston's employer announced in Baltimore, Maryland, that she was leaving the opera company to get married. She and Hurston would have to part ways, but Hurston was far from depressed. She later recalled,

It was not at all clear to me how I was going to do it, but I was going back to school. … I took a firm grasp on the only weapon I had—hope, and set my feet. Maybe everything would be all right from now on. Maybe. Well, I put on my shoes, and I started.[1]

New Beginnings in Baltimore

Twenty-six-year-old Hurston was determined to finish her high-school education, and a lack of money was not going to stop her. She heard about state laws that provided free schooling to people of color between the ages of six and twenty. Hurston lied about her age, saying she was just 16, to take advantage of the program.

Soon Hurston was enrolled in night classes. She so impressed teachers and administrators with her intelligence and obvious literary talent that they suggested she take her education a step further. Baltimore's Morgan Academy offered a high-school program in connection with Morgan College, known today as Morgan State University. Hurston was overjoyed at the prospect of attending the academy, but once again, she was concerned about money. Though she had been working as a waitress, she did not make enough to pay the private school's tuition costs. Luckily, the dean realized Hurston's potential. He and his wife made arrangements for her to work for and live with a prominent local white clergyman who had connections to Morgan.

Hurston's main responsibility was to look after the clergyman's wife, who was recovering from a broken hip. The work was easy, and the benefits were numerous. Hurston was compensated with two dollars a week, the luxury of not having to pay tuition, and housing that featured an impressive library. Though she began studies at Morgan with "only one dress, a change of underwear, and one pair of tan oxfords," her 17 classmates did not hold her poverty against her.[2]

The academy and college were African-American institutions. Many of her fellow students came from wealthy, well-known families in Baltimore's black social scene. But

"No Number Sense"

Though Hurston was undeniably a bright student, her grades revealed that she had a difficult time balancing her efforts between the subjects she adored and those she was less passionate about. She generally excelled in English, history, science, and music, but math consistently proved a sore point for her. Recalling one generous math instructor at Morgan, Hurston said, "I passed the courses because Professor Johnson, knowing that I did well in everything else, just made it a rule to give me a C. He probably understood that I am one of those people who have no number sense."[3]

despite the economic differences that may have separated them from Hurston, the young men and women at Morgan took a liking to her sharp wit and incomparable abilities in English. Not surprisingly, she excelled in classes that involved literature and writing, as well as subjects that sparked her curiosity or inspired her sense of creativity. As Hurston reflected in her autobiography,

> *My two years at Morgan went off very happily indeed. The atmosphere made me feel right. I was at last doing the things I wanted to do. Every new thing I learned in school made me happy.* [4]

By 1918, this happiness—combined with a stronger sense of confidence and purpose—convinced Hurston that very few of her dreams were unachievable. She would not be stopped simply because of an empty pocketbook, a lack of fancy

John Hurston's Death

John Hurston was killed when a train hit his car in Memphis, Tennessee, in 1918—the same year Zora left Baltimore with the hopes of enrolling at Howard. Sadly, Zora and her 57-year-old father had shared little contact since she had left Eatonville in 1911, and she was not present at his funeral.

dresses, or even her race or gender. Keeping this in mind, she directed her ambitions toward Howard University, an African-American college in the nation's capital.

"The Capstone of Negro Education"

Hurston later wrote that, "Howard University is the capstone of Negro education in the world. There gather Negro money, beauty, and prestige. It is to the Negro what Harvard is to the whites."[5] In June 1918, Hurston left Baltimore and headed to Washington, D.C. The bold move revealed her fierce desire for learning—approximately only 2,000 African Americans had been fortunate enough to attend any U.S. college the year before.

Hurston had to take additional preparatory classes before she was formally admitted, so she did not begin her university education until

An Important Influence

The support and encouragement of Hurston's teachers played a significant role in her determination to further her studies. Dwight O. W. Holmes was an especially important influence. Holmes taught Hurston English literature while she attended night classes (before her admittance to Morgan). He later taught at Howard and eventually became the university's first African-American president. Before Hurston could officially enroll at the university, she was required to take preparatory classes. At first, she was disappointed, but Holmes enthusiastically urged her to do so.

Hurston later remembered Holmes in her autobiography. "He never asked me anything about myself, but he looked at me and toned his voice in such a way that I felt he knew all about me. His whole manner said, 'No matter about the difficulties past and present, step on it!'"[6]

the fall of 1919. She kept up with tuition costs by working first as a waitress and later as a manicurist. Her earnings also allowed her to purchase a more fashionable wardrobe, which helped her fit in with the elegant and wealthy student population.

As was the case at Morgan, Hurston did not need too much assistance when it came to gaining acceptance from those around her. She was proud to be at Howard, and she worked hard to prove herself academically as she pursued a major in English. Her sense of humor, her remarkable mind, and her talent for composing poetry and short stories impressed her peers. Soon, Hurston was a member of a sorority and a campus literary club known as the Stylus. Through Stylus, Hurston met some of the city's most important writers. She even had the privilege to spend time with nationally recognized African-American authors such as W.E.B. Du Bois and James Weldon Johnson.

Surrounded by creative individuals who nurtured her gift for writing, Zora published the poem "O Night" and the short story "John Redding Goes to Sea" in 1921. Both pieces appeared in *The Stylus*, which was produced by the Stylus literary club. "John Redding Goes to Sea" not only represents Hurston's early attempts at authorship—it also contains many of the literary elements for which she would eventually become famous.

Her tale calls to mind the folklore, superstitions, and dialect that defined the African-American heritage of her Eatonville childhood.

The short story emphasizes her love of adventure and her appreciation for the unique qualities that played a role in the black culture of the South in the early twentieth century.

The publication of "John Redding Goes to Sea" and her first few years at

Early Indications of an Author's Style

In "John Redding Goes to Sea," John's father talks about his son, saying:

> dontcha know our boy is different from any othah chile roun' heah. He 'lows he's goin' to sea when he gits grown, an' Ah reckon Ah'll let 'im.[7]

Though fictional, the story features several of the same elements that shaped the author's early years in Eatonville. Like Hurston, John Redding has a passion for adventure and travel. Against the wishes of his mother and wife, he longs for a water voyage on Florida's St. Johns River.

Similar to the townsfolk who speckled her childhood with their exciting tales and magical folklore, John is also surrounded by men and women with a healthy respect for superstition. His world is filled with discussion of spells, witches, and foreboding signs that present themselves through pine trees and screech owls.

Just as important, however, is the manner in which the people who inhabit this world speak and convey their inner fears, thoughts, and desires. Dialogue is used to present a realistic portrait of black culture in the South. Hurston's word choice, expressions, and speech patterns imitate the speech patterns she heard growing up—and that she never forgot during her literary career.

Howard were important stepping stones in Hurston's growth as a writer. Unfortunately, however, they did not set the tone for her remaining time at the university. Hurston had become romantically involved with Herbert Sheen, another student, and was deeply saddened when he accepted a job in New York City in 1921. By 1923, she was doing poorly in several subjects and was struggling to pay tuition. In 1924, she was no longer taking classes at Howard.

Yet Hurston's recognition as an author was nowhere near its end. One of her professors had shared "John Redding Goes to Sea" with Charles S. Johnson, the editor of a New York-based magazine called *Opportunity: A Journal of Negro Life.* With the Harlem Renaissance well underway, the moment was right for a blossoming young writer such as Hurston to reveal her talent to a larger audience. ⌐

OPPORTUNITY

JOURNAL OF NEGRO LIFE

FEBRUARY **1926**

INDUSTRIAL ISSUE

Opportunity: A Journal of Negro Life *was one of the first places in which Hurston was published.*

In the 1920s, Harlem, an area of New York City, was the home of a black cultural explosion known as the Harlem Renaissance.

Harlem Renaissance Woman

y late 1924, Hurston remained in Washington, D.C., despite the fact that she was no longer a student at Howard. There was no doubt in her mind that she desired above all else to continue writing. Charles S. Johnson wholeheartedly supported her ambition.

After reading "John Redding," Johnson asked Hurston to submit another story for publication in *Opportunity*. Hurston's "Drenched in Light" tells the tale of an adventurous little girl from Eatonville named Isis Watts. The piece appeared in the magazine in December 1924—one month before Hurston heeded Johnson's advice and headed to New York City.

Hurston began her new life with no money, no job, and no place to stay. But shortly after she arrived in the African-American neighborhood called Harlem, she realized she had made the right decision. The cultural movement known as the Harlem Renaissance had begun there in about 1918, and the area was teeming with black writers, artists, musicians, and scholars. These men and women refused to allow their talent and intelligence to be blocked by racism. They delighted in an atmosphere filled with lectures, plays, concerts, parties, and debates—an atmosphere not readily available to blacks in most other parts of the country.

Hurston wasted no time in making her presence known in this world. With Johnson's help, she met and stayed with prominent Harlem residents who were eager to assist a new generation of promising young talent. She danced, attended social gatherings, and eagerly absorbed every bit of culture that her new environment had to offer. She also kept writing and submitted work to a contest sponsored by *Opportunity*. Though she may not have realized it, her literary efforts during her first few months in Harlem would pay off in ways she never would have imagined.

RECOGNIZED BY DIFFERENT RACES

Opportunity sponsored an awards dinner on May 1, 1925. Hurston was

The Lady Who Wanted Brightness

"The lady went on: 'I want brightness, and this Isis is joy itself, why she's drenched in light!'"[1] Like "John Redding Goes to Sea," "Drenched in Light" contains glimpses of Hurston's inner spirit and Eatonville childhood. It recalls those same elements with the help of the sassy, imaginative main character, Isis Watts. Like Hurston, Isis spends her youth dreamily watching travelers make their way down the road that runs past her home. And just as people had once admonished Hurston to accept the limitations of her race, Isis has a grandmother who tries to tame her bold personality.

When Isis sneaks off to a carnival, however, she impresses a white woman with her jubilant dancing. The lady ends up paying her surprised grandmother to see the little girl repeat the performance. In late 1924, when the story was published, Hurston was similarly shocking members of her own race with her accomplishments.

Whites of the academic and literary world as well as blacks of Harlem Renaissance fame were aware of Hurston and admired her accomplishments. Perhaps her true feelings were reflected when she wrote of her main character, "Isis for the first time in her life felt herself appreciated and danced up and down in an ecstasy of joy for a minute."[2]

thrilled by the prospect of winning. But more
importantly, the evening provided the opportunity
to spend time with notable men and women from
both races who represented wealth, power, and
talent. Famous writers such as Eugene O'Neill, Carl
Van Vechten, James Weldon Johnson, and Fannie
Hurst were in attendance. Annie Nathan Meyer was
also present. Meyer had helped found New York
City's prestigious Barnard College for women.

Up-and-coming African-American authors such
as Countee Cullen, E. Franklin Frazier, and Sterling
Brown all won prizes that night. Though Hurston
did not know Langston Hughes well at that time, he
was a winner, too. It would not be long before she
and Hughes would become close friends.

The name *Zora Neale Hurston* rang loudly on more
than one occasion as the dinner progressed. She
earned awards in the drama category for her play,
Color Struck, and in the fiction category for her short
story, "Spunk." Hurston could not have been more
pleased and proud, and those around her could not
help but take note of the intriguing young woman
who was gaining recognition at such a steady pace.

Meyer was especially impressed, and she offered
Hurston the opportunity to enroll at Barnard.

Words of Deep Gratitude

Having no surviving parents by 1925, Hurston found it refreshing to be the object of Annie Nathan Meyer's hopes and aspirations. It lifted her spirits and fueled her sense of ambition to know that another person was concerned about her future and proud of her accomplishments. As she wrote to Meyer in May 1925, "I am tremendously encouraged now. My typewriter is clicking away till all hours of the night. ... You see, your interest keys me up wonderfully. ... It is pleasant to have someone for whom one does things. It is [a] mighty cold comfort to do things if nobody cares whether you succeed or not. It is terribly delightful to me to have someone fearing with me and hoping for me, let alone working to make some of my dreams come true."[3]

Hurston rejoiced in the idea, but she was still worried about money. True, she had growing confidence that she could earn some income through her writing, but would it be enough to cover tuition? Hurston enrolled in the fall of 1925, but by the end of her first semester, she had her doubts.

Luckily, novelist Hurst admired her and intervened. She hired Hurston as her secretary and generously invited her to stay in her luxurious apartment. The arrangement was short-lived, though. Hurston disliked secretarial work, and Hurst was displeased with her attempts at it. Still, the pair remained good friends.

Hurst was a successful white author, and her friendship helped Hurston gain acceptance at the all-white college of Barnard. Students and teachers who had been aloof suddenly seemed to embrace her

Novelist Fannie Hurst encouraged Hurston's success at Barnard College.

upon discovering her connection to Hurst. As she later wrote to Hurst, "Your friendship was a tremendous help to me at a critical time. It made both students and faculty <u>see</u> me when I needed seeing."[4]

ARTISTIC CONTROVERSY

Thanks to a scholarship and occasional part-time jobs, Hurston managed to keep up with tuition costs at Barnard after she stopped working for Hurst. By 1926, she was busily shuffling between school and her apartment in Harlem. She was also attempting to balance her commitments. If she was not studying or working, she was fine-tuning her skills as a playwright, an essayist, and an author of short stories.

Her fascination with the black culture of the South continued to flourish, and she learned to masterfully insert humor and symbolism into her writing. Additionally, she remained dedicated to presenting African-American life as it really was. To Hurston, it was not critical that her characters always spoke in a manner that was grammatically correct. Nor did it concern her that her themes frequently centered on superstitions or folk wisdom that some might regard as foolish.

She was intent on revealing well-rounded individuals who experienced happiness and excitement, not just discrimination and failure. As she emphasized in her autobiography, "Negroes are just like anybody else. Some soar. Some plod ahead.

Some just make a mess and step back in it—like the rest of America and the world."[5]

Not everyone in Harlem agreed with her. Authors such as Du Bois felt that literature should educate others about the hardships blacks faced. Du Bois did not believe that it served blacks well to show them as superstitious or speaking improperly. Was this truly how blacks wanted whites to view them? Was this really how blacks viewed themselves?

Hurston and younger authors such as Hughes responded that artists should concentrate on the quality of their art. They need not be so concerned with furthering political or social arguments. Together with other young black artists, writers, and activists, they planned to publish an African-American magazine called *Fire!!* As the creators envisioned it, *Fire!!* would entirely focus on black art and literature, without any hidden propaganda.

Ironically, several copies of the original issue were destroyed in a fire in September 1926. At that point,

No Need to Impress

Hurston was well aware what an honor it was to be admitted to Barnard, and she was an enthusiastic learner. Yet she also decided that she was there to add to her own knowledge—not to impress the white student body and faculty. "I felt that I was highly privileged and determined to make the most of it," she explained. "I did not resolve to be a grind, however, to show the white folks that I had brains. I took it for granted that they knew that. Else, why was I at Barnard?"[6]

A Captivating Presence

Whether telling stories, dancing at parties, or simply entering a room, Hurston inevitably captivated those around her. Writer Arna Bontemps once noted after observing her in Harlem, "She was very outgoing. In any group she was the center of attention. ... In appearance, Zora was a pleasant, ordinary, brown-skinned young woman. Not stunning ... a little above average ... in appearance. But she had an ease and somehow projected herself very well orally. ... She didn't seem pushy or offensive in any way, but she somehow drew attention."[7]

Hurston and her collaborators lacked funds to pursue the project further. But Hurston remained determined to preserve the themes and styles already evident in her writing.

By the fall of 1926, 35-year-old Hurston was a fresh, powerful voice in the Harlem Renaissance, as well as a thirsty mind eager for the knowledge Barnard could offer. She was particularly intrigued by anthropology. Within a matter of months, her fascination with southern black folklore and her colorful memories of Eatonville would spur her in yet another direction on her amazing journey as an author.

Zora Neale Hurston in 1927

Anthropologist Franz Boas encouraged Hurston's work as a gatherer of southern folklore.

A CULTURAL EXPLORER

It was clear that Hurston's talents as an author defined her, but the Barnard student also excelled in anthropology. She especially admired Professor Franz Boas who, in turn, helped her gain funding from the university to study and collect the folklore of the black South.

Hurston clearly enjoyed New York and college life, and she had notably developed as a writer during the Harlem Renaissance. While at Barnard, she continued to publish stories and essays in various African-American magazines. Many of her efforts in 1926, including "Sweat" and "Muttsy," feature elements from her own life and childhood. *The Eatonville Anthology* features 14 shorter pieces all tied to her hometown.

Despite these literary successes, Hurston welcomed her new role as a gatherer of southern folklore. After purchasing a used car in Jacksonville— later to be called Sassy Susie—she headed home in February 1927. Unsurprisingly, she saw Eatonville as the perfect place to start. Yet, as she later confessed,

> *I did not have the right approach. The glamor [sic] of Barnard College was still upon me. I dwelt in marble halls. I knew where the knowledge was all right. But I went about asking, in carefully accented Barnardese, "Pardon me, but do you know any folktales or folksongs?" The men and women who had whole treasuries of material just seeping through their pores looked at me and shook their heads.* [1]

Boas was also disappointed with Hurston's early attempts at anthropology. Impressing her professor, however, was not the only challenge Hurston was up against. Six months of adventure lay ahead of her. The months were to be filled with danger, romance, and a search for her own identity as both a writer and an African-American woman.

Familiar Faces in an Unfriendly World

Hurston's skin color and gender made her an easy target for the racism that continued to cripple the South. More than a few whites were scandalized by a black woman rumbling along in her own car and forever asking questions and digging for details. At best, she was subject to an unwelcoming attitude, and she had to use public restrooms and water fountains specially designated for people of color.

At worst, she faced physical harm. In 1927, southern blacks often still lived in the shadow of

Telling Words

In May 1927, Hurston compiled a collection of idioms, or expressions, of the black South. These colorful idioms demonstrate the unique manner of speaking that she observed during her trip. They included:

- "Shut dat hash-pen (mouth)!"[2]
- "I'm walkin down de road wid de law in my mouf. (This woman [speaker] was very angry, determined, and heavily armed.)"[3]
- "You eats mocking bird eggs (tell everything you know)."[4]

A "white only" sign was a common sight in the South
that Hurston traveled through.

vandalism, beatings, and even murder. Ever since
the Civil War (1861–1865), whites and African
Americans had struggled to determine each race's
new role in society. Some people did not accept that
blacks should be treated equally. Some whites were
willing to do whatever was necessary to ensure that
they were not.

Regardless of how frightened she was, Hurston
made up her mind not to let racism discourage or
stop her. The Barnard student had much to do in a

very short time. Dwelling on the depressing reasons behind discrimination would only slow her down. Just as a precautionary measure, however, she carried a loaded pistol.

Luckily, the 1927 journey was not destined to be ruined by unspoken fears and hatred. In addition to gathering research, Hurston used her travels to reunite with the people she loved. In Memphis, Tennessee, she happily greeted brothers Bob and Ben and caught up on Hurston family affairs.

In May, she was back in Florida and had reconnected with sweetheart Herbert Sheen in St. Augustine. Now a medical student in Chicago, Sheen was eager to marry Hurston, and the two wed on May 19. Their romance proved short-lived. Sheen did not have much regard for Hurston's career, especially when he had one of his own to pursue back in the Midwest. Sheen and Hurston went separate ways soon after their wedding in 1927. In early summer, he departed for Chicago, while Hurston eagerly resumed her anthropological work in the South. The pair would ultimately divorce in 1931, though they led separate lives long before that date.

Hurston's next stop was in Mobile, Alabama, where she would be pleasantly surprised to find a reminder of happier days in Harlem.

A Traveling Companion

In Mobile, Hurston was overjoyed to bump into her New York friend Langston Hughes, who was also touring the South. Since the *Opportunity* awards dinner, Hurston and Hughes had become good friends. Between her disappointing marriage and frustrating efforts at gathering folklore, she welcomed the company of a fellow writer and member of the Harlem Renaissance. Hughes was likewise pleased at the prospect of heading back North with such an excellent tour guide.

Hurston did not disappoint her new traveling companion. Together, they lectured at Tuskegee Institute, a famous African-American college in Tuskegee, Alabama. They also visited

"A Moment Walking in Its Sleep"

Hurston's plans as a wife were somewhat advanced for the 1920s and proved a source of conflict with her new husband. During this era, many women did not strive for academically driven careers, and those who did often set them aside to raise a family after getting married.

Shortly after her wedding, Hurston realized that Sheen had little interest in helping her further her ambitions. Knowing that she was not suited simply to settling down and having children, she experienced bitter disappointment and disillusionment only a few days into her marriage. "I had an uncomfortable feeling of reality," she later wrote. "Who had cancelled the well-advertised tour of the moon? Somebody had turned a hose on the sun. What I had taken for eternity turned out to be a moment walking in its sleep."[5]

the grave of renowned black author and educator Booker T. Washington. They attended lively African-American church gatherings and strolled through picturesque Georgia plantations. They listened to blues performances by famous vocalist Bessie Smith and spent time with people who practiced hoodoo. This southern folk magic is rooted in a combination of various religions, including African spirituality, Christianity, voodoo, and an overall faith in the supernatural.

The Controversy of Cudjo Lewis

While in Mobile, Hurston interviewed a man named Cudjo Lewis, who was about 92 years old. Lewis was regarded as the last survivor of the final ship to bring slaves to U.S. shores. Hurston was stirred by his painful remembrances of the slave trade. "After seventy-five years," she recollected, "he still had that tragic sense of loss. That yearning for blood and cultural ties. That sense of mutilation. It gave me something to feel about."[6]

Unfortunately, Hurston's meeting with Lewis ultimately resulted in a controversy. The debate was linked to an article she wrote about him that was published in an African-American journal a few months after the interview. Decades after that, it was alleged that she had committed plagiarism by copying large chunks of text already included in another author's study of the former slave. Since these charges came to light after Hurston's death, they have never been fully explained.

Biographers have suggested that the text in question could have been the result of many causes, including footnotes getting lost in the mail. Perhaps Hurston never thought the article would actually be published, or perhaps she was pressed for time. No one knows whether her actions were intentional. Luckily, they never overshadowed the memory of her many contributions as a writer.

Hurston and Hughes were surrounded by the richness of African-American folktales and traditions. They excitedly wrote down and discussed what they heard and how it was said. As the pair drove along in Sassy Susie, their friendship deepened, as did their respect for each other's talent. By the time Hurston arrived back in New York in September 1927, she had abandoned her plans to collaborate on a novel with Hurst. Instead, she was eager to develop a folk opera with Hughes. Regarding him almost as a brother, she would later write, "Well, I tell you, Langston, I am nothing without you. That's no flattery either."[7]

Hurston's tour of the South may not have been successful in terms of her anthropology studies. Thankfully, the trip certainly would not be her last. Nor was the experience wasted. Though she admittedly needed to improve as a

Encounters along the Way

Hurston's and Hughes's travels could not be described as luxurious. Cash was tight for both writers. Besides, racial discrimination would have kept them out of many finer southern clubs, restaurants, and hotels, even if they had far more money. Additionally, Sassy Susie was plagued by a punctured tire and other mechanical troubles.

Nevertheless, Hurston and Hughes enjoyed talking with the locals they met along southern back roads. Sometimes these African Americans not only shared their stories but offered the pair home-cooked meals as well. Generally, such individuals were not wealthy and not necessarily impressed by claims of a college education. Hurston praised their simple, honest hospitality by describing them as "lovely people not spoiled by soap suds and talcum."[8] When she could get these men and women to open up, they proved essential in unlocking the culture and folklore of the black South.

researcher, the six-month journey left her with an even greater zest for southern black folklore. The words, expressions, and colorful spirit she witnessed both as a child of Eatonville and as a 36-year-old anthropology student shaped Hurston's portrayal of her race in writing. ⌐

Zora Neale Hurston, second from left, *with Langston Hughes,* center, *in 1927*

Zora Neale Hurston beats a drum as part of a hoodoo ritual.

NEW HORIZONS AND
UNEXPECTED FAREWELLS

While exploring the South with Hurston, Hughes had mentioned a lady named Charlotte Osgood Mason. The wealthy, elderly white woman acted as his patroness. She funded projects that he and other African-American artists, writers, and scholars might otherwise have been unable to pursue. Hughes was eager for Hurston and Mason to meet in the hopes that the aging widow could provide his dear friend with some much-needed financial assistance for her work.

The two women were introduced in September 1927 in New York City. By the following December, Hurston was on Mason's payroll. Hurston's assignment was:

> to seek out, compile, and collect all information possible, both written and oral, concerning the music, poetry, folklore, literature, hoodoo, conjure, manifestations of art and kindred subjects' among Negroes in the South.[1]

Mason, who swore Hurston to secrecy regarding their arrangement, was deeply fascinated with African-American culture. She was also impressed by the young black

A Low Blow

Charlotte Osgood Mason had an unpredictable temperament and could be a harsh and demanding patroness. She frequently reminded the people on her payroll that they were dependent upon her generosity, and she expected complete devotion and obedience. Hurston and Hughes often did not know how they had enraged her or what they could do to regain her favor.

Hurston felt Mason's wrath in early 1931 when the two women clashed over a discussion of finances. Mason coldly wrote that the author's attitude and actions were "the reason the whole white world says 'You can't do anything with Negroes. They are unreliable.'"[2] The accusation, though stinging, probably reaffirmed what Hurston already knew: Her employer may have been fascinated with black culture but, sadly, was not above expressing racist ideas.

author who signed a contract to conduct research for her. The terms of their agreement essentially compelled Hurston to devote the majority of her time and attention to her patroness. Additionally, the contract forbade her from publishing any of what she uncovered in her travels without Mason's permission.

Between late 1927 and early 1930, Hurston's new job took her from a lumber camp in Loughman, Florida, to hoodoo altars in New Orleans, Louisiana. She even braved hurricane winds to experience the scenic beauty and fascinating traditions of the Bahamas. During her journeys, she penned extensive notes and used a camera to record several reels of film. She did not make the same mistakes she had in Eatonville in early 1927.

This time, Hurston did not scare her subjects away by putting on the dignified airs of an accomplished college student. She effectively blended in with the culture she was observing.

Leaving Barnard

Hurston was conducting anthropological research in the South when it came time for her graduation from Barnard in 1928. Though she was not present at commencement, she had the distinction of being the college's first African-American graduate. Hurston's major was English. But she also minored in geology, the study of rocks as records of Earth's history.

In Florida, she sat in a cypress swamp with the lumberjacks as they indulged her with endless folktales. After heading to New Orleans, she served as an apprentice to several hoodoo doctors, and she enthusiastically joined in the energized folk dances. As Hurston wrote to Hughes from Florida in March 1928,

> I am truly dedicated to the work ... at hand and so I am not even writing, but living every moment with the people. I believe I have almost as many stories now as I got on my entire trip last year.[3]

When she returned to New York in early 1930, she was exhausted, but her research had been a success. Now that she was home, however, she was eager to collaborate with her good friend Hughes on a project that would leave a lasting mark on their once affectionate relationship.

A Painful Parting

In the winter of 1930, Mason made arrangements for Hurston to rent a room in Westfield, New Jersey. If the 39-year-old Hurston was sad not to have spent more time with her friends in Harlem, she was consoled by the fact that Hughes was one of

MULE BONE
ACT ONE
by
Zora Neale Hurston & Langston
Hughes

This play was never done because the authors fell out.

Langston Hughes

Agent for Mr. Hughes: Maxim Lieber, 545 Fifth Ave., New York, N.Y.

The title page from a draft of Mule Bone: A Comedy of Negro Life

her neighbors in Westfield. They delighted in each other's company and had even more in common now that both were working for Mason.

Though seemingly generous, the patroness sometimes proved moody, temperamental, and unpredictable when it came to providing support and approval. She was particularly annoyed by Hurston's and Hughes's joint efforts on a play titled *Mule Bone: A Comedy of Negro Life*, based on one of Hurston's short stories set in Eatonville. As far as Mason was concerned, she was paying Hurston to produce manuscripts based on her findings from the previous two years. Mason was irritated that the pair had not asked her permission to pursue another project.

Nevertheless, Hurston and Hughes continued their creative partnership. They were often aided by a secretary named Louise Thompson, who eventually became the center of the argument that forever changed their friendship. When Hughes suggested that he and Hurston give Thompson one-third of the play's profits and make her the business manager, his coauthor

End of a Renaissance

When Hurston lived in Harlem during the 1920s, not all her acquaintances were wealthy. But most were pleased and proud to be part of a vibrant community where literature, art, and opportunity flourished. As early as 1930, however, she sensed a change in the neighborhood's atmosphere, as well as the attitude of its residents. With the country in the grip of the Great Depression, jobs were scarce and poverty was far-reaching. As Hurston wrote to literary representative Lawrence Jordan in the early summer of 1930, "I was in Harlem yesterday for the first time. Some of my friends are all tired and worn out—looking like death eating crackers. All of them cried to me to come and put some life into the gang again."[4]

angrily objected. It was not long before Hurston and Hughes were quarreling over which writer had contributed more to the play and who had greater rights to it.

Soon threats of legal action flew back and forth. Hurston returned to New York in June 1930, and the once inseparable friends grew colder and more uncompromising. In the end, *Mule Bone* never made its way to the stage. Just as disappointing was the bitter end of a dynamic, adventure-filled relationship. Years

A Real-life Drama

Hurston and Hughes initially planned to base much of *Mule Bone* around a short story Hurston had written called "The Bone of Contention." This comedic tale takes place in Eatonville and focuses on two hunters—Dave and Jim—fighting about who shot a wild turkey. During the dispute, Jim assaults Dave with an old mule bone. Their disagreement carries over into the village, ultimately involving supporters from each man's respective church. In the end, Jim is ordered not to return to Eatonville for two years.

Though Hughes suggested occasional changes to the plot, Hurston remained adamant that she had played a greater role in creating the dramatic work. "It was my story from beginning to end," she wrote him in January 1931. "It is my dialogue, my situations. But I am not concerned about that."[5] However, the question of authorship and rights—as well as the level of Thompson's involvement—all had devastating effects on Hurston's friendship with Hughes.

The pair periodically attempted to resolve their hostility, but their efforts consistently failed. Though Hurston acknowledged that "both of us got worked up unnecessarily," the damage was done.[6] *Mule Bone* would never gain theatrical acclaim while they lived, and she and Hughes would never truly reconcile.

later, Hurston would still regret her parting from Hughes, referring to it as "the cross of her life."[7]

DRAWN TO THE STAGE

By early 1931, Hurston and Hughes were no longer close, and she was officially divorced from Herbert Sheen. Throughout these personal challenges, however, she remained focused on advancing her career as a playwright. Technically, her contract with Mason had ended by 1930. However, her former employer still occasionally loaned her much-needed money and words of encouragement to pursue new creative efforts.

Hurston did not require much prompting. After composing a series of short skits for African-American variety shows, she went on to write *The Great Day*. The folk musical called upon her 1928 experiences in a Florida work camp. The play, which was later renamed *From Sun to Sun,* opened in New York in January 1932. The performance—which ranged from African-American sermons to lullabies to work songs—was well received by critics but failed to bring in substantial ticket sales.

Hurston found herself locked in a difficult situation. Lacking a steady paycheck, she was eager to continue her writing but was struggling to make ends meet in a changing society. The Harlem Renaissance had been drawing to a close in the early 1930s, partly as a result of the Great Depression. Men and women of all races lost their jobs and homes. They no longer had the luxury of attending poetry readings and helping to further art and literature. Even with her considerable talent, Hurston had difficulty paying her rent in New York.

She begged Mason to provide her with the means to return to Eatonville, where it was cheaper to live. Her wish granted, Hurston headed to her hometown in the spring of 1932. She still had not completed the book of folklore based on her research from between 1927 and 1930, but she seemed optimistic about the move. Writing to Mason shortly before departing New York, she noted, "Somehow a great weight seems lifted from me."[8] Whether that weight was a failed friendship or the fading promise that the Harlem Renaissance had offered her race, it was removed from Hurston's shoulders. Once unburdened, she would take her career in a direction that the literary world would never forget.

Zora Neale Hurston in New York City, around 1935

A manuscript page from Hurston's most famous novel,
Their Eyes Were Watching God

FOLKLORE FICTION
AT ITS BEST

urston's escape to Florida in 1932

was exactly what she needed to refresh

herself and focus on her craft. As she wrote to

Charlotte Osgood Mason in May, "I am happy here,

happier than I have been for years. … The clang

and clamor of New York drops away like a last year's dream."[1] In the quiet peace of a small rented house with a garden, Hurston completed work on her folktales, ultimately naming the collection *Mules and Men*.

She also started thinking about new and creative ways to present the flavor of black folk culture to the people of Florida. During the next few years, she worked with local colleges and various dramatists to organize concerts and shows. They featured everything from African-American spirituals to hoodoo dances. All the while, however, money problems continued to plague her. The country was still feeling the effects of the Great Depression, and it was especially hard for African Americans to find profitable work.

Mason initially mailed a small monthly allowance, but her contact with Hurston quieted as the elderly patroness began to suffer from health problems. Desperate to make rent, Hurston tried to get a teaching job at Bethune-Cookman College in Daytona Beach, Florida, but the African-American school had no openings. With no steady funding, her expenses began to multiply. Though Hurston collaborated with faculty at Rollins College in Winter

Park, Florida, to produce her popular concerts, she still ended up using some of her own money to fund the shows.

Luckily, a professor at Rollins College took interest in a short story Hurston had completed in 1933. He passed "The Gilded Six-Bits" along to respected *Story* magazine, and Hurston's name appeared on the August edition of that publication. Her heartwarming and true-to-life tale of a young African-American couple earned her $20. Just as importantly, she caught the attention of several big-name publishers who inquired if she had any longer fictional pieces. Inspired by this response, Hurston headed to Sanford, Florida. In a less familiar and therefore less distracting setting, she could concentrate on writing the novel that she had long dreamed of creating.

Jonah's Gourd Vine

In October 1933, Zora shipped *Jonah's Gourd Vine* to J. B. Lippincott Company, a major publisher. The novel is a fictional retelling of her parents' lives. It features the same unashamed representations of southern black culture that are trademarks of Hurston's work from the 1920s. Yet, she wondered if her style and point of view were appropriate for Lippincott. As she later reflected,

> From what I had read and heard, Negroes were supposed to write about the Race Problem. I was and am thoroughly sick of the subject. My interest lies in what makes a man or a woman do such-and-so, regardless of color.[2]

Lippincott agreed with Hurston's point of view. On October 16—just hours after she had been evicted from her home for failing to pay rent—she opened a telegram from Lippincott. The publisher wanted to move ahead with her manuscript and offered her a $200 advance payment. Thrilled at the taste of success, Hurston readily accepted the terms of the publishing agreement.

It would be seven months before *Jonah's Gourd Vine* was released, and it was clear that she would need more money before then. From

Writing with No Apologies

Hurston was well aware that whites were accustomed to seeing African-American characters portrayed as downtrodden by a racist world. She also realized that several black writers and critics did not want to stray from this formula because they believed it made society aware of a great injustice.

Hurston was not about to adjust her style or message to accommodate either whites or African Americans. As she wrote to former mentor Fannie Hurst of *Jonah's Gourd Vine*, "It may not be literature, but it certainly is sincere work. ... It is from the middle of the Negro out—not the reverse. ... I do not attempt to solve any problems. I know I cannot straighten out with a few pen-strokes what God and men took centuries to mess up. So I tried to deal with life as we actually live it—not as sociologists imagine it."[3]

Thrill of a Lifetime

On October 16, 1933, Hurston was in a shoe store when she finally opened the telegram that bore Lippincott's acceptance of her manuscript for *Jonah's Gourd Vine*. As she later recalled, "When I opened it and read that ... Lippincott was offering me a $200 advance, I tore out of that place with one old shoe and one new one on and ran to the Western Union office. Lippincott had asked for an answer by wire [by telegram], and they got it! Terms accepted. I never expect to have a greater thrill than that wire gave me."[5]

January through April 1934, Hurston was employed by Bethune-Cookman College. Founder and president Mary McLeod Bethune had given her the responsibility for establishing a drama school. Unfortunately, Hurston subsequently realized she required more time to revise the folktales in *Mules and Men*, which Lippincott had also agreed to publish. In addition, she had discovered she easily clashed with Bethune, so her resignation and retreat to Longwood, Florida, in mid-April came as a welcome relief.

When *Jonah's Gourd Vine* was unveiled just a few weeks later, the public was largely impressed with the book's language and well-rounded, believable characters. One admirer at *The New York Times Book Review* reported,

> [It] can be called without fear of exaggeration the most vital and original novel about the American Negro that has yet been written by a member of the Negro race.[4]

Some reviewers—even those who shared her African-American heritage—were less kind. They questioned why she would "write a novel about a backward Negro people, using their peculiar speech and manners to express their lives."[6]

This, of course, had not been Hurston's goal. Regrettably, her determination to reveal blacks as realistic men and women who shared the same hardships and happiness as people of any other skin color was frequently misunderstood. But critics' doubts regarding her literary intentions did not stop her from further writing and certainly did not slow her down. Her greatest achievement as an author was yet to come.

THEIR EYES WERE WATCHING GOD

During 1934 and 1935, Hurston could not seem to stay put, first taking up residence in Chicago and later heading back to New York City. She briefly attended graduate classes in anthropology at Columbia University and resumed some of her research in the South. Amazingly, she still managed to find time to perform her famous folk concerts and to write a sampling of articles, short stories, and essays for various publications. Beginning in October 1935, she spent six months working as a drama coach in New York. That same month, she also absorbed the response to the release of *Mules and Men*.

As with *Jonah's Gourd Vine*, many reviewers acknowledged and praised Hurston's abilities as a folklorist. Yet some African-American authors and critics bristled at her depiction of black southerners, as well as her choice of topic and use of dialect. Were the magical animals and

---

The Life Lessons of Janie Crawford

Hurston may not have always used her novels as platforms for social messages, but her themes do often touch upon certain issues such as racism and gender equality. In *Their Eyes Were Watching God*, Janie Crawford is an African-American woman within a society where some people believe a woman's ultimate goal should be to marry well or work for a respectable white family. Janie creates her own sense of independence by overcoming various struggles and experiencing different kinds of love. She survives what the world has thrown at her and retells her tale from her Eatonville porch.

Like Hurston herself, Janie copes with both the rewards and the hardships of reality to live life to its fullest on her own terms. She refuses to allow her skin color or gender—or the expectations people set for her—to slow her down. As Janie remarks to her friend,

> Ah'm back home agin and Ah'm satisfied tuh be heah. Ah done been tuh de horizon and back and now Ah kin set heah in mah house and live by comparisons. ... Two things everybody's got tuh do fuh thevselves. They got tuh go tuh God, and they got tuh find out about livin' fuh thevselves.[7]

fantastic elements she included relevant considering all the injustices her race faced? Such rebukes frustrated Hurston. However, she was not about to accommodate those individuals who preferred to only read about sad, unsuccessful blacks left hopeless amidst violence and segregation.

Nor did she choose to shake off the "travel dust" that her mother once complained had been sprinkled on their doorstep. In the spring of 1936, she was awarded $2,000 to study African culture and magic in the West Indies. Hurston eagerly set forth for Haiti and Jamaica. She spent seven weeks writing with remarkable intensity under what she subsequently described as "internal pressure."[8] The result of her labor was a novel that was considered by many to be her best.

Their Eyes Were Watching God is the love story of a woman named Janie and a much younger man called Tea Cake. Though racism plays a role in the characters' lives, the text unsurprisingly devotes greater attention to the characters themselves. Published in September 1937, the novel triggered some unfavorable criticism from Hurston's African-American peers. But it was more overwhelmingly met with enthusiasm and appreciation for her use of

A Writer's Regret

Hurston later claimed that she was not completely satisfied with *Their Eyes Were Watching God*—or any of her work. As she recounted in her autobiography, "I wish that I could write it again. In fact, I regret all of my books. It is one of the tragedies of life that one cannot have all the wisdom one is ever to possess in the beginning."[10]

dialect and the passion with which she breathed life into Janie, Tea Cake, and their Eatonville setting. Even normally harsh reviewers emphatically deemed the book "folklore fiction at its best."[9]

In February 1938, on the heels of such acclaim, Zora headed to her hometown to craft a manuscript based on her research from the West Indies. At 47, she had successfully interwoven her name with other world-famous authors of different racial backgrounds. But it was not time for Hurston to rest yet. She was still in need of work, money, and an outlet to satisfy her never-ending cravings for adventure and creative expression of black culture.

The original cover of Their Eyes Were Watching God, *1937*

Zora Neale Hurston in 1938

THE END TO A
STORYTELLER'S STORY

By the late 1930s, Hurston had achieved recognition as a talented—if sometimes misunderstood—novelist. Still, she could by no means claim the wealth that most white authors enjoyed. The decade following her return to Florida was filled with a variety of jobs designed to help make ends meet and still allow her to pursue her writing.

From May 1938 to August 1939, she was a member of the editorial staff at the Federal Writers' Project (FWP) in Jacksonville, Florida. The FWP was associated with the Works Progress Administration (WPA), one of many government programs designed to help U.S. citizens recover from the Great Depression. Hurston was invited to assist with a history of African-American life and culture of Florida. Her contributions included folklore, folk music, and several essays from black myths to games and dances.

In the spring of 1938, she finished her book on the West Indies. Published in the fall as *Tell My Horse*, it left critics impressed with Hurston's descriptions and obvious enthusiasm for Haiti and Jamaica. Yet several reviewers also remarked that her writing lacked focus and organization.

If Hurston was disappointed by this feedback, the whirlwind changes in her personal life may have helped distract her. In June 1939, she married 23-year-old Albert Price III. The union quickly proved unhappy and ended in divorce just four years later. In the meantime, Zora began teaching drama at the North Carolina College for Negroes in Durham, North Carolina.

In November 1939, she published a third novel—*Moses, Man of the Mountain.* A retelling of the life of the Old Testament character, the book subtly addresses issues related to race, slavery, and clashing cultures. But once again, several of her African-American readers missed many of these themes. Or if they did not, they nonetheless criticized that her messages were not strong or obvious enough.

Hurston was dejected by this response and became disappointed in her own work. By March 1940, she left her teaching post at the college and buried herself in anthropological research, turning to the black culture of South Carolina. Later that year, she briefly returned to New York and accepted another assignment from J. B. Lippincott. She soon departed for California to better concentrate on the task ahead of her. But this particular manuscript would not require her to go any further than her personal memories.

FINAL WORK, FINAL DAYS

Hurston's stay on the West Coast in 1941 and 1942 was a busy, exciting time. She had the

opportunity to work with the
Paramount Pictures film studios as
a writer and consultant—a unique
achievement for an African-
American woman during the 1940s.
She was also crafting her latest piece
for Lippincott—an autobiography
titled *Dust Tracks on a Road*. In her
original version, Hurston expressed
many honest and somewhat radical
opinions on topics ranging from the
U.S. government to racism. With the
United States entering World War II
in late 1941, however, her publisher
was convinced that the timing was not
right to include ideas that were likely
to upset the public.

Though heavily edited, the book
proved highly popular upon its
release in November 1942. Hurston
appeared on magazine covers, and
she received numerous awards. She
had returned to Florida earlier
that year to earn extra income as
a summer literature professor at

Freedom Is Internal

Moses, Man of the Mountain touches upon broad issues such as race and freedom. It also reinforces Hurston's personal belief that no culture or country is ideal—that it is up to individuals to shape their lives.

In the novel, Moses liberates the Hebrews from slavery under their Egyptian masters, but he ultimately concludes that there is no such thing as a good or bad race, just good or bad people. The narrator notes toward the end of the book, "He [Moses] had meant to make a perfect people, free and just, noble and strong, that should be a light for all the world and for time and eternity. And he wasn't sure he had succeeded. He had found out that no man may make another free. Freedom was something internal."[1]

the Florida Normal and Industrial College in St. Augustine. But once her autobiography fell into reviewers' hands, she was suddenly busier than ever meeting publishing deadlines for new projects.

By 1943, she moved to Daytona Beach, Florida, and eventually purchased a houseboat. Hurston focused on refining her journalism skills by writing essays and articles pertaining to race relations. She briefly married Ohio businessman James Howell Pitts in January 1944, but they divorced eight months later. The next few years were destined to be filled with difficulty and frustration.

Hurston split her time between Florida and New York, and she quickly found her expenses mounting. This was worsened by her realization that Lippincott was unenthusiastic about her proposed novels. Her publisher seemed reluctant to take on work featuring characters who strayed too far from African-American stereotypes. "There is over-simplification of the Negro," she complained in 1944. "He is either pictured … as happy, picking his banjo, or … low, miserable and crying."[2]

Hurston's spirits were temporarily uplifted when an editor at Charles Scribner's Sons, a major publisher, offered her a book contract in April

1947. Finally, she had the money to fulfill her dream of exploring the culturally rich Central American country of Honduras from May 1947 to February 1948. Unfortunately, her return was tarnished by false accusations that she had abused a group of children from her neighborhood in Harlem. Though the charges were ultimately dismissed, they left Hurston deeply depressed. Even the success of her final novel *Seraph on the Suwanee*, which was published in October 1948, did not lift her depression.

In 1949, a series of short stories, essays, and book

Different Races, Similar Ways of Speaking

Several of Hurston's novels feature African Americans as central characters, but *Seraph on the Suwanee* focuses on a poor, white Florida couple named Arvay and Jim Meserve. Despite this shift in race, dialect still plays an important role in the book. Through her research, Hurston discovered that whites and blacks who called the same region of the South home and who came from less wealthy, prominent backgrounds also shared ways of speaking.

As she later explained to a friend,

About the idiom of the book, I too, thought that when I went out to dwell among the poor white in Dixie County that they were copying us. But I found their colorful speech so general that I began to see that it belonged to them. ... I realized that Negroes introduced into N. America spoke no English at all, and learned from the whites. Our sense of rhythm points it up a bit, but the expressions for the most part are English held over from the Colonial period. ... Just stand around where poor whites work or around the village stores of Saturday nights & listen & and you will hear something.[3]

A "Magnificent Character"

Hurston was eager to release a novel about biblical King Herod the Great. In the New Testament, the ruler murders several Hebrew children in an attempt to destroy the infant Jesus. Despite Herod's horrific reputation and editors' apparent disinterest, Hurston was intrigued by the ruler. As she observed in a letter to Charles Scribner's Sons in 1953, "No matter who talks about him, friend or foe, Herod is a magnificent character. … It came to me that a character does not have to be lovable to make good reading. Some of the most popular books and plays have been built around detestable characters."[4]

reviews helped pay her bills, but this financial stability was brief. The aging author was still unable to retreat into a world where her creativity and talent were not upstaged by worries of poverty. By 1950, her books were out of print, and publishers were less eager to accept her manuscripts. Shifting from one Florida town to the next, Hurston spent 1950 to 1958 employed as a librarian, a substitute teacher, and even a maid. There is a famous story about how the wealthy, white owner of a Florida mansion unexpectedly discovered the true identity of her domestic helper. The woman was shocked to learn that the famous African-American writer she was reading about in the *Saturday Evening Post* was the same woman who was cleaning her home.

Despite her setbacks, Hurston refused to completely abandon her craft. She contributed articles and commentaries on important events of the day. These included the Ruby McCollum trial, in which a black woman was charged with murdering a white physician, and the 1954 verdict in *Brown v. Board of Education.* This landmark Supreme Court decision effectively ended segregation in public schools.

In 1957, Hurston was invited to join the newspaper staff of the *Fort Pierce Chronicle.* Once relocated to Fort Pierce, Florida, she befriended several of the other *Chronicle* writers and editors. She even found a home where she was allowed to live free of rent once the landlord, who admired Hurston and knew her Eatonville family, discovered how poor she actually was.

But hardship remained. Hurston continued to receive rejection letters from publishers who either no longer saw the appeal of her name or who were unwilling to tackle the projects she hoped to undertake. She also suffered from heart disease and became largely dependent on welfare for food and medications. In October 1959, she had a stroke and was admitted to a county nursing home. Though she remained cheerful and as independent as possible, she suffered a second stroke on January 28, 1960.

That winter evening marked the final moments of the 69-year-old author's life.

THE SUM OF LIFE

While newspapers across the country spread word of Hurston's death, her friends and colleagues rallied to collect money to pay for her funeral. When she was buried in Fort Pierce on February 7, there still were not enough funds to include a headstone at her gravesite. Services were attended by more than 100 mourners—men and women, blacks and whites, wealthy and poor—the same mixture of people who Hurston had impressed and astounded during her lifetime.

Yet it was not this remarkable show of respect that breathed new life into her work. In the summer of 1973, writer Alice Walker visited Hurston's final resting place in Fort Pierce. As a gesture of reverence

A Tribute by Alice Walker

Alice Walker is a famous African-American author perhaps best known for her 1982 novel, *The Color Purple*. Walker writes of the struggles and ultimate triumphs of a black woman living in Tennessee. Impressed by Hurston's accomplishments and eager to honor her legacy, Walker once remarked, "We love Zora Neale Hurston for her work first, and then again (as she and all Eatonville would say), we love her for herself. For the humor and courage with which she encountered a life she infrequently designed ... and for her devoted appreciation of her own culture, which is an inspiration to us all."[5]

Zora Neale Hurston's play Polk County *was performed at the Arena Stage in Washington, D.C., in 2002. The play was rediscovered several decades after Hurston's death.*

for Hurston's talent and amazing existence, Walker marked her grave with a headstone that bears the words "Zora Neale Hurston: A Genius of the South."[6] Walker followed up her visit with an essay about Hurston in the popular *Ms.* magazine, and a renewed wave of interest in Hurston's work began.

By the late 1970s and early 1980s, her books were back in print. Her name and accomplishments were referenced in countless publications, and biographers eagerly retold her story. Plays she had composed but never had been produced—including *Mule Bone*—made it to the stage with much acclaim. The woman who had defied barriers connected to money, gender, and race had also defied obscurity in death.

Whether remembered as a folklorist, novelist, anthropologist, dramatist, or journalist, Hurston is considered one of the finest authors of the twentieth century. She may not have foreseen how valuable her contributions to literature ultimately would be deemed, but she lived each day enthusiastically and with an excitement about where her abilities and ambitions would take her. As she once said,

> What waits for me in the future? I do not know. I cannot even imagine, and I am glad for that. But already, I have touched the four corners of the horizon, for from hard searching it seems to me that tears and laughter, love and hate, make up the sum of life.[7]

Today, Zora Neale Hurston is regarded as one of the most significant American authors.

TIMELINE

1891

Zora is born in Notasulga, Alabama on January 7.

1904

Zora's mother dies on September 18. Weeks later, Zora is enrolled at Florida Baptist Academy.

1919

Hurston enrolls at Howard University. She subsequently gains exposure to prominent authors in Washington, D.C.

1927

In September, Charlotte Osgood Mason becomes Hurston's patroness.

1928

Hurston officially receives a degree in English from Barnard College on February 29. She is the school's first African-American graduate.

1930

Hurston and Langston Hughes collaborate on a play called *Mule Bone: A Comedy of Negro Life* but quarrel over rights to the dramatic work.

1925

Hurston begins study at Barnard College in New York City in September. She soon becomes an active force in the Harlem Renaissance.

1927

Under the instruction of Professor Boas, Hurston sets out in February to spend six months collecting southern black folklore.

1927

Hurston marries college sweetheart Herbert Sheen in St. Augustine, Florida, on May 19.

1931

Hurston and Sheen divorce in July.

1932

The musical *The Great Day* (later renamed *From Sun to Sun*) opens in New York in January. It is met with enthusiastic reviews but poor ticket sales.

1934

Jonah's Gourd Vine receives favorable reviews, though some critics question Hurston's lack of attention to racial oppression.

TIMELINE

1935

Mules and Men is published and receives praise—and criticism—similar to *Jonah's Gourd Vine.*

1937

Their Eyes Were Watching God is published and earns widespread praise.

1938

Tell My Horse is published. Critics respond favorably to Hurston's descriptive writing but judge the piece to be unfocused.

1943

Hurston and Price divorce in November.

1944

Hurston marries James Howell Pitts in January; they divorce in October.

1948

Hurston's final novel, *Seraph on the Suwanee,* is released in October to largely positive reviews.

1939

Hurston marries Albert Price III in June.

1939

Moses, Man of the Mountain is published in November. Hurston is deeply disappointed by black critics' unfavorable reviews.

1942

Hurston's autobiography *Dust Tracks on a Road* is released in November. It proves highly popular.

1950–1958

Extreme financial hardship forces Hurston to accept part-time work as a librarian, a substitute teacher, and a maid.

1960

Hurston dies at the age of 69 on January 28.

1973

Alice Walker's essay about Hurston in *Ms.* magazine inspires a renewed interest in Hurston's life and work.

Essential Facts

Date of Birth

January 7, 1891

Place of Birth

Notasulga, Alabama

Date of Death

January 28, 1960

Parents

John Hurston and Lucy Anne Potts

Education

Florida Baptist Academy, Jacksonville, Florida; Morgan Academy, Baltimore, Maryland; Howard University, Washington, D.C.; Barnard College, New York City, New York

Marriages

Herbert Sheen (1927–1931), Albert Price III (1939–1943), James Howell Pitts (Jan.–Oct., 1944)

Residences

Hurston moved and traveled frequently, living in many places along the East Coast and Caribbean Islands, including Florida, Maryland, New Jersey, New York, and North Carolina.

SOCIETAL CONTRIBUTIONS

Hurston desperately pursued an education and became the first African-American graduate of Barnard College. She traveled throughout the southern United States collecting folklore for her work in anthropology, and she saw her dramatic work produced on stage. Hurston never compromised her ideals as an artist.

PERSONAL CONFLICTS

Hurston struggled to finish her education with little family support and money. Finding money and free time to write plagued her until her death. Hurston also struggled to find lasting love and was married and divorced three times. She also suffered a falling out with fellow writer Langston Hughes. Though Hurston saw fame in her lifetime, she also felt limited by critics, who wanted her to focus more on social issues affecting African Americans.

KEY WORKS

"John Redding Goes to Sea," short story, published in *Stylus*, 1921; "Drenched in Light," short story, published in *Opportunity: A Journal of Negro Life*, 1924; *The Great Day* (renamed *From Sun to Sun*), folk musical, opened 1932 in New York City; *Mules and Men*, a collection of folktales, 1935; *Jonah's Gourd Vine*, novel, 1934; *Their Eyes Were Watching God*, novel, 1937; *Tell My Horse*, firsthand account of Hurston's experiences with voodoo in Haiti and Jamaica, 1938; *Moses, Man of the Mountain*, novel, 1939; *Dust Tracks on a Road*, autobiography, 1942; *Seraph on the Suwanee*, novel, 1948

QUOTE

"Negroes are just like everybody else. Some soar. Some plod ahead. Some just make a mess and step back in it—like the rest of America and the world." —*Zora Neale Hurston*

ADDITIONAL RESOURCES

SELECT BIBLIOGRAPHY

Boyd, Valerie. *Wrapped in Rainbows: The Life of Zora Neale Hurston*. New York: Scribner, 2003.

Hurston, Lucy Anne. *Speak, So You Can Speak Again: The Life of Zora Neale Hurston*. New York: Doubleday, 2004.

Hurston, Zora Neale. *The Complete Stories*. New York: Harper-Perennial, 1996.

Hurston, Zora Neale. *Dust Tracks on a Road: An Autobiography*. New York: HarperCollins Publishers, 2006.

Hurston, Zora Neale. *Moses, Man of the Mountain*. Urbana and Chicago: University of Illinois Press, 1984.

Hurston, Zora Neale. *Their Eyes Were Watching God*. New York: Harper-Collins Publishers, 2000.

Kaplan, Carla, ed. *Zora Neale Hurston: A Life in Letters*. New York: Anchor Books, 2002.

The Library of Congress American Memory Project—Today in History (January 7): Zora Neale Hurston. <http://www.memory.loc.gov/ammem/today/jan07.html>.

FURTHER READING

Bryant, Philip S. *Zora Neale Hurston*. Chicago: Raintree, 2003.

Cannarella, Deborah. *Zora Neale Hurston: African American Writer*. Chanhassen, MN: Child's World, 2003.

Litwin, Laura Baskes. *Zora Neale Hurston: "I've Been in Sorrow's Kitchen."* Berkeley Heights, NJ: Enslow Publishers, 2005.

Myers, Christopher, ed. and illus. *Lies and Other Tall Tales (Collected by Zora Neale Hurston)*. New York: HarperCollins, 2005.

Thomas, Joyce Carol, ed. and Bryan Collier, illus. *What's the Hurry Fox? and Other Animal Stories (Collected by Zora Neale Hurston)*. New York: Harper Collins, 2004.

Web Links

To learn more about Zora Neale Hurston, visit ABDO Publishing Company on the World Wide Web at **www.abdopublishing.com**. Web sites about Zora Neale Hurston are featured on our Book Links page. These links are routinely monitored and updated to provide the most current information available.

Places to Visit

Zora Neale Hurston Dust Tracks Heritage Trail
3008 Avenue D, Fort Pierce, FL 34947
772-462-1618
www.st-lucie.lib.fl.us/zora

Walk a trail to commemorate Hurston's impact on St. Lucie County, Florida, where the writer spent her final years. The trail includes her house and the site of her funeral.

Zora Neale Hurston National Museum of Fine Arts
227 East Kennedy Boulevard, Eatonville, FL 32751
407-647-3307
www.zorafestival.com/museumhome.html

See exhibits of African and African-American art.

GLOSSARY

anthropology

The study of human cultures.

conjure

To summon spirits.

dialect

Use of vocabulary particular to a specific culture or group of people.

discrimination

Unequal treatment of a person that is often based on gender, religion, or race.

domestic laborers

Workers such as maids and cooks who are employed to help clean a house or care for its residents.

dramatist

A playwright.

folklore

The traditions, stories, songs, sayings, beliefs, or customs particular to a specific culture or group of people that are often passed down from generation to generation.

Harlem Renaissance

A period during the 1920s and 1930s when African-American art and culture flourished in New York City.

hoodoo

A type of folk magic in the South rooted in a combination of various religions, including African spirituality, Christianity, voodoo, and an overall faith in the supernatural.

idioms

Words and expressions that have an understood meaning within a particular culture.

Jim Crow laws

> Laws that existed from the late nineteenth century until the 1960s that favored discrimination and segregation.

lynch

> To kill a person (often by hanging) without the authority of the law.

mentor

> A teacher or a counselor who often uses his or her knowledge and experience to guide or instruct a younger person.

patroness

> A woman who offers financial support to members of the artistic community.

philanthropist

> A person who uses his or her time and money to help others.

plagiarism

> Copying another person's work and presenting it as one's own.

prominent

> Important or well-known.

propaganda

> The use of the media and public communication to promote social or political messages.

segregated

> Giving separate or unfair treatment and opportunities to people based on gender, religion, or race.

sharecroppers

> Farmers who rent the land they work on and usually pay the owner with a portion of their crops.

Source Notes

Chapter 1. The Lure of the Lying Sessions
1. Zora Neale Hurston. *Dust Tracks on a Road: An Autobiography*. New York: HarperCollins Publishers, 2006. 48.
2. Ibid. 46.
3. Ibid. 52.
4. Valerie Boyd. *Wrapped in Rainbows: The Life of Zora Neale Hurston*. New York: Scribner, 2003. 142.
5. Ibid. 145.
6. Ibid. 144.
7. Lucy Anne Hurston. *Speak, So You Can Speak Again: The Life of Zora Neale Hurston*. New York: Doubleday, 2004. 18.
8. *Preservation: A Brief History*. 15 May 2007. The Association to Preserve the Eatonville Community, Inc. (P.E.C.). 15 May 2007 <http://zorafestival.com/preservationhome.html>.
9. Lucy Anne Hurston. *Speak, So You Can Speak Again: The Life of Zora Neale Hurston*. New York: Doubleday, 2004. 28.
10. Ibid. 25.

Chapter 2. Roots of a Remarkable Imagination
1. Zora Neale Hurston. *Dust Tracks on a Road: An Autobiography*. New York: HarperCollins Publishers, 2006. 22-23.
2. Ibid. 27.
3. Ibid. 13.
4. Ibid. 13.
5. Ibid. 19.
6. Ibid. 39.
7. Ibid. 58.
8. Ibid. 30.

Chapter 3. Learning Harsh Lessons
1. Zora Neale Hurston. *Dust Tracks on a Road: An Autobiography*. New York: HarperCollins Publishers, 2006. 13.
2. Ibid. 67.
3. Ibid. 67.
4. Ibid. 70.
5. Ibid. 70.
6. Ibid. 71.
7. Ibid. 84.

8. Ibid. 87.
9. Ibid. 84.
10. Ibid. 100.
11. Ibid. 88–89.

Chapter 4. Eager for an Education
1. Zora Neale Hurston. *Dust Tracks on a Road: An Autobiography*. New York: HarperCollins Publishers, 2006. 119.
2. Ibid. 126.
3. Ibid. 129.
4. Ibid. 129.
5. Ibid. 129.
6. Ibid. 124.
7. Zora Neale Hurston. *The Complete Stories*. New York: HarperPerennial, 1996. 3.

Chapter 5. Harlem Renaissance Woman
1. Zora Neale Hurston. *The Complete Stories*. New York: HarperPerennial, 1996. 25.
2. Ibid. 25.
3. Carla Kaplan, ed. *Zora Neale Hurston: A Life in Letters*. New York: Anchor Books, 2002. 55.
4. Ibid. 85.
5. Zora Neale Hurston. *Dust Tracks on a Road: An Autobiography*. New York: HarperCollins Publishers, 2006. 140.
6. Ibid. 252.
7. Valerie Boyd. *Wrapped in Rainbows: The Life of Zora Neale Hurston*. New York: Scribner, 2003. 99.

Chapter 6. A Cultural Explorer
1. Zora Neale Hurston. *Dust Tracks on a Road: An Autobiography*. New York: HarperCollins Publishers, 2006. 143–144.
2. Carla Kaplan, ed. *Zora Neale Hurston: A Life in Letters*. New York: Anchor Books, 2002. 98.
3. Ibid. 98.
4. Ibid. 99.
5. Zora Neale Hurston. *Dust Tracks on a Road: An Autobiography*. New York: HarperCollins Publishers, 2006. 204.

Source Notes Continued

6. Ibid. 168.
7. Carla Kaplan, ed. *Zora Neale Hurston: A Life in Letters*. New York: Anchor Books, 2002. 155.
8. Valerie Boyd. *Wrapped in Rainbows: The Life of Zora Neale Hurston*. New York: Scribner, 2003. 152.

Chapter 7. New Horizons and Unexpected Farewells
1. Valerie Boyd. *Wrapped in Rainbows: The Life of Zora Neale Hurston*. New York: Scribner, 2003. 159.
2. Carla Kaplan, ed. *Zora Neale Hurston: A Life in Letters*. New York: Anchor Books, 2002. 204.
3. Zora Neale Hurston. *Dust Tracks on a Road: An Autobiography*. New York: HarperCollins Publishers, 2006. 144.
4. Valerie Boyd. *Wrapped in Rainbows: The Life of Zora Neale Hurston*. New York: Scribner, 2003. 207.
5. Carla Kaplan, ed. *Zora Neale Hurston: A Life in Letters*. New York: Anchor Books, 2002. 252.
6. Ibid. 202.
7. Ibid. 113.
8. Valerie Boyd. *Wrapped in Rainbows: The Life of Zora Neale Hurston*. New York: Scribner, 2003. 216.

Chapter 8. Folklore Fiction at Its Best
1. Carla Kaplan, ed. *Zora Neale Hurston: A Life in Letters*. New York: Anchor Books, 2002. 254.
2. Zora Neale Hurston. *Dust Tracks on a Road: An Autobiography*. New York: HarperCollins Publishers, 2006. 171.
3. Carla Kaplan, ed. *Zora Neale Hurston: A Life in Letters*. New York: Anchor Books, 2002. 286.
4. Valerie Boyd. *Wrapped in Rainbows: The Life of Zora Neale Hurston*. New York: Scribner, 2003. 257.
5. Zora Neale Hurston. *Dust Tracks on a Road: An Autobiography*. New York: HarperCollins Publishers, 2006. 175.
6. Valerie Boyd. *Wrapped in Rainbows: The Life of Zora Neale Hurston*. New York: Scribner, 2003. 258.
7. Zora Neale Hurston. *Their Eyes Were Watching God*. New York: HarperCollins Publishers, 2000. 225–226.
8. Zora Neale Hurston. *Dust Tracks on a Road: An Autobiography*. New York: HarperCollins Publishers, 2006. 175.

9. *Review by Alain Locke*, Opportunity, *1 June 1938*. 2 Nov. 2006. The University of Virginia Library/Electronic Text Center. 16 June 2007 <http://etext.lib.virginia.edu/railton/enam854/summer hurston.html>.

10. Zora Neale Hurston. *Dust Tracks on a Road: An Autobiography*. New York: HarperCollins Publishers, 2006. 175.

Chapter 9. The End to a Storyteller's Story

1. Zora Neale Hurston. *Moses, Man of the Mountain*. Urbana and Chicago: University of Illinois Press, 1984. 344.

2. Valerie Boyd. *Wrapped in Rainbows: The Life of Zora Neale Hurston*. New York: Scribner, 2003. 379.

3. Carla Kaplan, ed. *Zora Neale Hurston: A Life in Letters*. New York: Anchor Books, 2002. 577–578.

4. Ibid. 702.

5. Alice Walker, ed. *I Love Myself When I Am Laughing … and Then Again When I Am Looking Mean and Impressive*. New York: The Feminist Press, 1979. 2.

6. *Zora Neale Hurston: Bold, Brave, and Beautiful*. 14 Nov. 2003. Phi Theta Kappa: International Honor Society of the Two-Year College. 14 June 2007 <http://www.ptk.org/publications notabene/99authors/reysim99.htm>.

7. Zora Neale Hurston. *Dust Tracks on a Road: An Autobiography*. New York: HarperCollins Publishers, 2006. 265.

INDEX

About the Author

Katie Marsico writes children's books from her home near Chicago, Illinois. She lives with her husband and their two children. Before beginning her career as an author, Marsico worked as a managing editor in children's publishing.

Photo Credits

Library of Congress, cover, 3, 6, 13, 14, 28, 43, 64, 84, 96 (top), 99 (bottom); Lightfoot/Getty Images, 16; Yale Collection of American Literature, Beinecke Rare Book and Manuscript Library, 23, 33, 53, 63, 68, 73, 74, 83, 95, 96 (bottom), 98, 99 (top); AP Images, 24, 49, 57; Corbis, 34; Underwood & Underwood/Corbis, 44; Bettmann/Corbis, 54, 97; Scott Suchman, Arena Stage/AP Images, 93